# THE NORTH
# COTSWOLDS
## IN OLD PHOTOGRAPHS

FOUR SHIRE STONE, two miles east of Moreton-in-Marsh at the traditional meeting place of Gloucestershire, Oxfordshire, Warwickshire and Worcestershire. The first three counties still border here, although the Worcestershire connection disappeared during reorganisation in the early 1930s when Evenlode parish was transferred into Gloucestershire. Built in Cotswold stone, the pillar is completed by a sundial and a ball finial.

# THE NORTH
# COTSWOLDS
## IN OLD PHOTOGRAPHS

COLLECTED BY
# DAVID VINER

ALAN SUTTON
1988

Alan Sutton Publishing Limited
Brunswick Road · Gloucester

First published 1988

**British Library Cataloguing in Publication Data**

The North Cotswolds in old photographs.
1. England. Northern Cotswolds.
I. Viner, D.J. (David James), *1947–*
942.4'17

ISBN 0-86299-441-1

**Cover illustration:** EBENEZER BAPTIST CHAPEL in Blockley, built in 1835 and presenting a fine
classical façade to the faithful approaching through the churchyard from the High Street.
The Baptist tradition was strong in Blockley with six of the seven leading mill-owners in the
community in the 1850s as members. Blockley's eminent Baptist Richard Boswell Belcher
is seen standing by his wife's grave. He was a keen champion of social causes and died in
1901. Out of use for regular services since around 1971, the chapel is now converted for
domestic use.

Typesetting and origination by
Alan Sutton Publishing Limited
Printed in Great Britain
by WBC Print Limited

# CONTENTS

'Century after century everything here has been unhurried, quiet and orderly, and time could have been measured rather by the dial than the ticking of the clock. On the town, year after year has fallen and has left no more trace than have last winter's snowflakes'

Lord Sankey speaking of Moreton-in-Marsh at the opening of the town's new post office on 1 December 1933.

Most of the photographs in this volume are the work of local photographers, whose efforts in recording the local scene have been rescued from obscurity by collectors motivated by the same desire to preserve the local story for posterity. The particular diligence of local history groups in Moreton-in-Marsh and Blockley is recorded in the Acknowledgements, and so too the individual collections from which much of the material for the Longborough, Chipping Campden and several other sections has been drawn. It is possible to see the influence of particular photographic studios in a compilation such as this and wherever possible the source of each photograph is noted in the hope that this might assist future study. All group identifications should be read from left to right.

The work of Butt Studio of Bourton-on-the-Water will be apparent throughout, linking this volume with the companion *Northleach to Stow-on-the-Wold in Old Photographs* in the same series (1987) where the history of the studio is summarised. Other studios include Clift & Ryland of Stow, J.W. Farrell also of Stow, Frank Packer and Percy Simms ('The Packer Studio') of Chipping Norton, Henry Taunt of Oxford and Chapman & Co. of Blockley. Also for Blockley, the work of the local studio of Sirett is noted on page 78. Most, if not all, of the Chipping Campden material seems to come from the studio of Tom Taylor, photographer and watchmaker.

The photograph above shows Moreton-in-Marsh butcher Charles Drury with his Christmas display of 1923. The family butchery business began in Moreton in 1817 (moving from Aston sub Edge) and remains one of the oldest businesses in the town. Charles' second son Reg Drury rescued much of the Moreton material in this volume to form the basis of a local history collection for the town (Butt of Bourton).

# INTRODUCTION

When the first photographers appeared, the Cotswolds were at the nadir of their reputation. The great days of the wool industry in the late Middle Ages were as much ancient history as they are today, though isolated flocks of the old breed of Cotswold sheep could still be found on the uplands. This did not mean, however, that the people of the district were necessarily despondent or discontented. It meant that, as far as the country at large was concerned, the Cotswolds were a quiet backwater, where people lived in old-fashioned houses built of the local stone.

Today, the district is regarded as the epitome of rural England. Cotswold architecture is admired and copied far beyond the topographical limits of the area. In any list of tourist attractions, the Cotswolds would be near the top and the growth of interest in the district has led to a local revival of traditional crafts with the emphasis on personal workmanship. The Cotswolds are, in fact, more famous today than they have been for several centuries though their fame now rests on the guide book instead of the woolsack.

Indeed, tourism probably vies with farming as the major industry of the district. During the past century, Cotswold farmers have seen more years of depression than prosperity, but during recent decades have enjoyed a measure of security. The revolution caused by the introduction of machines has made Cotswold farms more productive than they have ever been. This revolution has, however, had its effect on local employment: farms can now manage on a fraction of their former labour force and many who would once have worked on the land must look elsewhere for employment. Stone quarrying has long been an alternative outdoor occupation locally.

The only industrial village in the north Cotswolds has been Blockley, where a silk industry was established at the beginning of the eighteenth century. Disaster struck in 1860 when the Government concluded a trade treaty with France which removed the 30 per cent tariff protecting silk manufacturers. By August of that year all eight mills in Blockley, employing 800 people, were closed and poverty stalked the village. A few years later, two or three mills were re-opened during the Franco-Prussian war, but the silk industry in Blockley never really recovered and was dead by 1900. Some of the old mills have now been converted into attractive homes.

The latter half of the nineteenth century saw several prominent buildings erected in the north Cotswolds, including the Redesdale Hall (1887) and Mann Institute (1891) at Moreton. The Old Grammar School in High Street, Chipping Campden, was enlarged and almost totally rebuilt in 1865 and later on, Campden Town Hall was also extended. A cottage hospital was built at Moreton in 1873, one of the earliest of its kind in the country. Meanwhile the district was well-served by the Great Western Railway with stations at Campden, Blockley, Moreton and Adlestrop. Gas companies were formed at Moreton in 1846 and Campden in 1869.

Gas was soon to find a rival in electricity when, in 1887, Blockley made history by becoming the first village in England to have electric light. A powerful lamp was placed on the church tower which was said to shed a glow like moonlight over the village streets. The presence of water power made this innovation possible, the sponsor being Lord Edward Spencer Churchill, of Northwick Park, whose kinsman, Nigel Warburton, was in charge of the project.

During the closing years of the last century, the first tourists began to trickle in, artists painted Cotswold scenes and picture postcards appeared in the shops. An influential event occurred in 1902 when the Guild of Handicrafts moved from London to Campden with the avowed aim of producing honest craftsmanship in carving, joinery, metalwork, jewellery, etc., without the aid of machines. This not only had an effect on the town but also attracted further interest from outside and soon there was a resident coterie of artists and writers whose work did much to familiarise the public with the Cotswold tradition.

In 1931, changes were made to the county boundaries and those islands of Worcestershire, which included Blockley, were in due course transferred to Gloucestershire and in 1935, a North Cotswold Rural District Council was formed to administer the district. An annual competition for the best-kept village in Gloucestershire, the first of its kind in the world, was inaugurated by Viscount Bledisloe and at least one town or village in the North Cotswolds features among the winners each year. Moreton has one of the loveliest cricket grounds in the

Cotswolds, where the great Dr W.G. Grace once batted and where county matches are still held; Blockley has an admirably sited bowling green and Campden has its famous 'Cotswold Olympicks', played each year on blustery Dover's Hill above the town.

The North Cotswold and Heythrop Hounds have regularly met in the district and the presence of so much first-class hunting stock has contributed towards the success of the Moreton and District Agricultural and Horse Show, now one of the biggest one-day shows. It was established in 1949 following the amalgamation of the old Moreton Horse Show and Moreton Agricultural Societies and the Cotswold Agricultural Society, which had been in existence for over a hundred years.

The sun that was setting on the old rural hierarchy shone brightly at Moreton in 1905 when the popular King Edward VII visited his friend, Lord Redesdale, at Batsford Park. The king was given an enthusiastic reception on his arrival at the railway station and during his coach rides round the district. A delightful incident occurred at Campden when the king stopped and bought a paper from a local news-vendor, Bob Dickenson, who thereafter carried the royal coat-of-arms on his satchel.

A symbolic incident which presaged a revolution in country life occurred near Moreton in 1901. 'Mr Tarplett, the baker, lost his grey mare on Thursday afternoon,' reported the local newspaper on 17 August that year. 'The mare was with the cart at Batsford when a motor car came round a corner and the mare was so frightened that she turned round and fell dead.' By her reaction, the grey mare must have realised that this strange machine signalled the doom of her race as a means of road transport. The coming of the internal combustion engine opened up the Cotswolds to a much greater number of visitors. Situated within an easy afternoon's drive of the tourist centres of Stratford-upon-Avon, Oxford and Cheltenham, the district became a popular target for motorists and charabanc tours. The old coaching inns took on a new lease of life with the advent of motor travel and the North Cotswolds have numerous excellent hotels.

It was in the years between the two world wars that the great Cotswold street markets came to an end. At one time there was no more familiar sight in the district than the broad main street, crowded with livestock in pens and farmers buying or selling. When traffic grew heavier these markets were transferred to adjacent, purpose-built sites: however, the broad Cotswold streets, though no longer serving their original purpose, soon became useful as spacious traffic parks.

To an outsider, it is the unchanging quality of the Cotswolds that is their greatest charm. Here, he feels, is a part of the English countryside whose beauty and character have escaped the clumsy hand of time. Yet the Cotswolds have changed considerably during the past century though not as conspicuously as other regions may have done. The towns and villages have not altered essentially nor has the landscape with its network of stone walls and dome-shaped clumps of beech trees. It is in the way of life of the inhabitants of the district — their opportunities for learning, travel and more comfortable living — that the greatest changes have occurred and, hopefully, many of these changes are reflected in the photographs chosen for this volume.

Contributed by David Day
Moreton-in-Marsh.

LONGBOROUGH BELL RINGERS early this century. At the rear are T. Pethrick, A. Williams and S. Green and in the foreground A. Spragg, T. Williams and A. Partington.

# SECTION ONE

# Moreton-in-Marsh

MORETON-IN-MARSH HIGH STREET in the 1920s looking south towards Stow-on-the-Wold. The wide main street is a characteristic of Cotswold market towns, seen also at Campden elsewhere in this volume, and discernable still in the market squares of Stow, Cirencester, Fairford, etc. Here the periodic street fairs were held, particularly of sheep and cattle, removed only in fairly modern times to purpose-built sale yards away from the growing volume of traffic.

Moreton's main street has a Roman origin. It follows the line of a major cross-country road of Roman Britain, the Fosse Way, running diagonally across the country – and the Cotswolds – from south-west to north-east. The later street layout along this earlier spine is largely medieval, dating from the founding of the 'new town' in the thirteenth century. There are market grants dating from 1226 and 1228 and the name 'old town', for that part of Moreton clustered around the parish church, is evidence of the earlier settlement.

Nineteenth-century Moreton enjoyed something of a population growth with improved communications, particularly the arrival of the railway in 1853. It remains on a major road link for visitors to the area, denying views such as this of a large open central area uncluttered by vehicles for most of the year.

This view also shows the Redesdale Hall, opened in 1887 and Moreton's most conspicuous building. It was built for the town in commemoration of the first and last Earl Redesdale – John Thomas Freeman Mitford – who inherited the nearby Batsford Estate from his father and lived there as a bachelor until his death in 1886. His cousin and successor Algernon Bertram Freeman Mitford built the Hall in his memory.

In this century, parish teas in the Hall were very popular between the wars, forming one of the highlights of the Moreton calendar. When the centenary of the 22 December 1887 opening was celebrated recently, this tradition of teas and the subsequent concert and dance were also repeated.

(Butt of Bourton, postmarked August 1932)

MORETON HIGH STREET in an earlier view and looking north, believed to be c. 1864. The later imposition of the Redesdale Hall upon this wide street can be appreciated. In the group of buildings on the right is Horne's original grocers shop and Moreton's oldest town business. Further up on the corner of East Street is the town pound where straying animals were kept for collection on payment of a fee.

MORETON TOWN CROSS, demolished around 1850 but recorded here in a drawing by John Powell c. 1805. On the right is the Curfew Tower, one of the town's oldest surviving buildings from which the bell was regularly rung as a curfew until 1860. Its last bell ringer was William Webb who died in 1862. His other duties included town crier, parish constable, church sexton, parish beadle and bill sticker.

THE BATSFORD ESTATE DONKEY CART in Moreton at the top end of the High Street, photographed in the 1890s by Hon. David Mitford, later the second Baron Redesdale. Note the fine line of trees on both sides of the road, planted by the same Mitford who built the Redesdale Hall and intended to provide a suitable setting for it. Most of the trees were removed in the 1950s although those on the left still survive on the greens.

ANOTHER VIEW OF THE REDESDALE HALL with the Redesdale Arms Hotel on the left, formerly the Unicorn Hotel. The ground-floor arcading has since been filled up.

MORETON FAIR & MARKET DAY C. 1906. Sheep were sold in the High Street, cattle on the Green and pigs at the rear of the Redesdale Arms Hotel. In 1923 a new market was opened near the railway station (see page 33). In this view, the informal style of the street market can be appreciated along with a fine display of shop frontages behind.

MARKET DAY AGAIN and perhaps a year or two later. Here the cattle are waiting to be sold, the men looking knowledgeable and the boys always ready with a stick to help things along (Chapman of Blockley, postmarked 1909 and sent as a birthday greeting to Charles Drury Esq – see page 6).

CURFEW TOWER at the junction of High Street and Oxford Street. It is probably sixteenth century and is now a designated ancient monument. In the tower is a bell dated 1633 and the clock has a date of 1648. A faded inscription reads: 'Sir Robert Fry, Gent. gave 10s. for ringing the bell and 20s. a year to keep this clock in order.' The building was also used as the town lock-up and the toll-board records the market tolls. The Curfew Tower was restored in 1982/3 (Chapman of Blockley postmarked 1908).

THE MANN INSTITUTE was built in 1891 by Miss Edith Mann in memory of her father Dr John Mann on the site of some demolished cottages and his birthplace. It was intended as a working men's club with hall, reading room and billiards room, together with a library for which purpose it has been used until recently. Redesdale Hall stands behind in the High Street. In the foreground is one of the farm wagons of Albert Brassey Esq., of Dunthrop.

THE PLOUGH INN OR PACKHORSE INN and subsequently part of University Farm at the southern end of the High Street, as recorded in another of Powell's illustrations of c. 1805. The date 1678 above the doorway forms part of an attractive leaf ornament moulding.

LONDON ROAD in Moreton, taken from roughly where the Wellington Inn is now. Ciceter Terrace shows in profile on the left and straight ahead are Mitford Villas. The London Road council houses on the right had yet to be built. Pye's Britannia Works, also on the right, began in more modest circumstances at the railway wharf, but here manufactured iron window casements. The building continues in use for commercial purposes (Packer of Chipping Norton).

ST DAVIDS PARISH CHURCH photographed between 1858–60 after the rebuilding of the church and before the modest sixteenth-century tower was replaced by a larger tower and spire. The oldest part of the town clustered around the earlier church on this site.

BATSFORD TURN at the northern end of the High Street and just before the railway bridge. The cottage is a former turnpike toll-house, well situated to command the traffic at this junction.

ANOTHER VIEW TOWARDS THE HIGH STREET from the railway bridge, with the road to Batsford leading off to the right (postmarked 1905).

MORETON STATION STAFF in an undated group photograph. On the right is the old 'up' platform with its siding and nameplate for the former Shipston tramway. In 1826 a horse-drawn tramway was opened between Moreton and Stratford, with a branch to Shipston-on-Stour, to link with the Stratford Canal. From 1889 the tramway was converted for use by steam trains and continued in use as a branch line until the late 1950s.

Moreton Station was opened on 4 June 1853 on the Oxford, Worcester and Wolverhampton Railway line from Oxford to Worcester. The station is at the highest point on the railway system between London and Worcester, Moreton being close to the watershed between the Thames and Severn river basins.

The OW & WR was absorbed by the Great Western Railway in 1863 and in the following years a number of the original wooden stations on the line were rebuilt. At Moreton this happened in 1872/3 with the construction of a four-bay building in yellow brick with red and black string courses. It survives today and so too does the rail service to Worcester, Oxford and London.

Note the publicity board for the 'White Hart Royal Comercial Hotel and Posting House' in the High Street.

KING EDWARD VII visited his friend Lord Redesdale at Batsford Park from 8–10 July 1905, arriving by train at Moreton station. He is seen leaving there in the photograph above. This visit of a reigning monarch created great interest, reflected in the lower photograph in the High Street with crowds awaiting the King's carriage *en route* to Batsford from the station (lower photo: Chapman & Co. Series, Blockley).

FOLLOWING THE DEATH OF KING EDWARD VII a memorial service was held in Moreton together with a procession along High Street on 20 May 1910 (Percy Simms, Chipping Norton).

CELEBRATORY BUNTING outside the Bell Hotel and all the main shops in the High Street for the coronation of King George V.

STRONG BROS WORK FORCE OF TAILORS on 1 December 1933, the day the town's new post office was opened. Strongs long held a reputation as the premier tailor of quality for the town and indeed the north Cotswolds generally. Standing are: Cyril Gilson, Percy Strong, Robert Sharp , Harry Strong and Horace Hine. Seated are: Jim Bowden, Eddie Garrett, Percy Garrett, Arthur Franklin, Charlie Garrett, Jack Pethard, Tom Winstone, William Bennett, Billy Oliver, Ernest Nevitt, Frank Slatter, Jack Barrington and Arthur Perry (Butt of Bourton).

MR F.W. BEW stands in front of his grocery and hardware shop in High Street, Moreton, in a photograph taken around 1935. Largely unaltered on the ground floor, the premises remains a hardware shop today. Note the board advertising sausages at 1s. per lb.

HEYTHROP HUNT MEETS in Moreton, thirty years apart. The upper view is postmarked 11 April 1906 (Chapman & Co. Series, Blockley); the lower view is 1936 outside the Redesdale Arms Hotel, which was often the scene of meets of the Heythrop. Known as the Unicorn before 1891, it was one of Moreton's principal coaching inns (together with the White Hart) in the late eighteenth century and dates from that period (Frank Packer of Chipping Norton).

THE UNVEILING of the Moreton and Batsford war memorial designed by Sir Guy Dawber on 26 March 1921. The ceremony was performed by the second Baron Redesdale of Batsford Park who succeeded to the title in 1916. The Redesdales had sold the estate in 1919 when ownership passed to Sir Gilbert Alan Hamilton Wills of the tobacco family, later created first Baron Dulverton. Accordingly, he also took part in the ceremony and is seen in the lower photograph standing centre nearest to the memorial. In the background, Strong's shop links with page 23 (lower photo: Percy Simms of Chipping Norton).

HOSPITAL FÊTE on Bank Holiday Monday 1908, parading in a field off the Batsford Road. Proceeds benefited the cottage hospital. Here the Tradesmen's Turnout is being judged between Ernest Teague (ironmonger), Arthur Price (butcher) and Charles Drury (butcher).

COTTAGE HOSPITAL founded in the town in July 1873 and opened with due ceremony. The initial seven beds were increased together with other facilities over the years as fund raising allowed ('M.P.C.' Series).

EXTENSIONS TO THE COTTAGE HOSPITAL were opened in both 1925 and in 1935. In this ceremony (?1925) local benefactress Mrs Arthur Dugdale performs the honours accompanied by Lord Dulverton, committee president and another great benefactor standing on her left. Hospital secretary Arthur Drury stands between them. On the extreme left is Dr Clark Nicholson, standing next to J.A. Riddey (Percy Simms of Chipping Norton Four Shires Series).

HOSPITAL STAFF photographed on 15 January 1936. The matron is Miss Ockenden who subsequently married Dr Nicholson. Seated beside her is Miss Mary Barrett, later Mrs Cecil Grimes of Moreton (Frank Packer of Chipping Norton).

POST OFFICE BAND photographed outside the post office (postmarked 1909)

PARISH FÉTE held on the cricket field on 24 June 1908 (Chapman of Blockley).

ANOTHER FÊTE, this time in 1914 (Frank Packer of Chipping Norton).

SEWAGE PUMPING STATION under construction in London Road c. 1907.

THE FIRE BRIGADE was formed in around 1896 with the manual pump housed in several places before a new building was provided in East Street in 1925. In this view c. 1905 the brigade members are (at the rear): C. Betheridge, R. Beddoes & ? Milton. In the centre: driver E. Gray, G. Miles, ? Webb and ? Nelson. In front: F. Gray, F. Clayton, H. Warden, J.W. Coppage and A. Timms. The boy is Bert Clayton (Percy Simms of Chipping Norton).

THIS RECONDITIONED MERRYWEATHER MOTOR FIRE ENGINE was purchased in 1935 which was the Jubilee year of King George V. By this time only Fred Clayton (standing left) remained of the original 1896 crew. He received the Silver Medal of the National Union of Fire Brigades for 20 years' service (Butt Studio, Bourton-on-the-Water).

THIS LINE-UP at a Second World War demonstration brings together the fire brigades from Moreton (on the left) and Blockley (on the right) with the third unit probably from Stow. At least two of these volunteer units attended the air raids on the city of Coventry (Butt of Bourton).

MORETON INFANTS SCHOOL in 1921, Back row: Bob Sharp, Winnie Strong, George Tombs, -?-, Eileen Oliver. Second row; Fred Young, Ted Madgwick, Marjorie Jones, Molly Talbot, L. Blythe, Nancy Dyer. Seated: Ivy Jones, Emma Franklin, Gladys Hardiman, Winnie Mills, Marjorie Drury, Joan Drury, Betty Nelson, Vernon Abell, Elsie Dyer, George Hardiman. In the front row: Peter Young, Tommy Tustin, Harry Strong, Monica Bryan, Gladys Jeffrey and Les Hooper.

MORETON GIRL GUIDES on parade in 1921 (Butt of Bourton).

Moreton Comrades' Féte 16-5-21. - Tug-o'-War.

Butt, Bourton & Stow.

Little Lemington Team- Winners.

9.

MORETON COMRADES FÊTE held on 16 May 1921. This is the Little Lemington team, winners of the tug-o'-war competition. The group includes members of local families: Stinton, Marshall, Harvey and Spragg (Butt of Bourton).

OPENING OF NEW SALEYARD AT MORETON-IN-MARSH

A NEW SALEYARD WAS OPENED IN NEW ROAD in January 1923 to reduce congestion in High Street. Auctioneers Bosley & Harper of Shipston-on-Stour purchased the tolls and market rights from Lord Dulverton, who as Sir Gilbert Wills (as he then was) performed the opening ceremony.

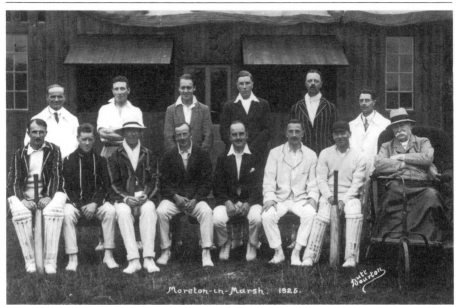

MORETON HAS ONE OF THE MOST BEAUTIFUL CRICKET GROUNDS IN THE COUNTY. The great W.G. Grace played there and county matches continue to be held at Moreton. Included in this 1925 team picture are (back row): Percy Sheen, D. Timms, Sydney Mace, Tony Beck, -?-, and ? Harris. Front row: C.J. Hull, -?-, Dr Holbrook, L. Horne, Arthur Drury, Percy Strong, Tom Strong and, in the chair, Henry Rouse. The occasion was the opening of the new cricket pavilion (Butt of Bourton).

MORETON GLEE SOCIETY lined up at a gathering. Is anything more known about this club and its activities?

A PROUD DISPLAY BY MORETON TOWN FC after a very successful 1930–31 season during which they triumphed in the first division of the Cheltenham League, and carried off the Bourton Hospital Cup and the Moreton Hospital Cup. The goalkeeper is Jim Allen (Butt of Bourton).

THE DAIRY in Moreton has an interesting history in premises on the north side of the railway line near the station. Attempts at running a co-operative dairy locally date back to 1889, but the major development on this site was undertaken by the United Dairy Company which ran a modern and prosperous business for some years.

However, resulting from a dispute over the price of milk to producers, a number of landowners and farmers co-operated in 1922 to form a Direct Dairy Co-operative Company, with Col. Dugdale of Sezincote as chairman. Mr Glover of Aston Magna as managing director and Mr Harold Shepard of Aston Hale as secretary. This co-operative traded successfully for a decade, during which time the United Dairy Company closed its doors. The co-operative had its headquarters in both Moreton and London. In 1931 it declared a trading loss for the first time in its history.

In 1932 the Retail Mutual Dairy Company purchased the premises of both companies and started business as the Mutual Dairies Ltd. This photograph shows the party present on the occasion of the completion of purchase of the premises on 31 March 1932. They are from the left : W. Woodall, Capt. B.P. Hornby, M.C., ?, H. Shepard, R.O. Clover, H.A. Wright, FRIBA, T. Rowlands, M. Jones, B.C. Marsh, E. Prestage, F.J. Williams, D. Owen, G. Hardy (president of R.D. Mutual Ltd), D.E. Jones, E. Jones, J.W. Lomas, W.H. Crawshaw, H.B. Hill, I.B. Whitehouse, S.F. Barnes, A.R. Ash, F. Hawes and D.E. Davies.

Mutual Dairies had a large business which grew so that 36 local people were employed and 30 lorries used for collections. In January 1937 the company was incorporated into United Dairies Ltd. of London.

The station overbridge can be seen in the background.

Opening of New P.O. at Moreton by Lord Sankey. 1-12-33. (1)

THE OPENING OF THE NEW POST OFFICE in New Road on 1 December 1933, performed by Moreton's most illustrious son, Viscount Sankey, who was the Lord Chancellor. He was born at Wellington House in Evenlode Road in 1866. On his left is W.S. Morrison, MP for Cirencester and Tewkesbury, who later became Speaker of the House of Commons and was then created first Viscount Dunrossil. Also on the platform are C.A. Jackson, Post Office District Surveyor, Col. Arthur Dugdale, chairman of the Moreton magistrates, Brig.Gen, R.A. McCalmont, chairman of the Glos County Highways Committee, F.W. Harrison, chairman of Moreton Parish Council, W.H. Ludlow the architect and R.C. Hall, Head Postmaster of Evesham. A celebratory lunch followed at the White Hart Royal Hotel (Butt of Bourton).

Luncheon to Lord Sankey of Moreton. 1-12-33. (4.)

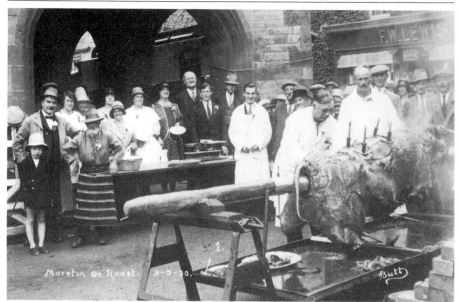

AN OX ROAST AND PLEASURE FAIR in the High Street was an important fund-raising occasion for the cottage hospital. Money was collected for the purchase of the ox which was then dressed and fastened to a pole to be roasted whole in front of a fire. Here on 9 September 1930 Will Dyer supervises operations outside the Redesdale Hall (Butt of Bourton).

THE SAME GATHERING five years later in 1935, with, in the white coats, Charles Drury, Wiliam Dyer, Cecil Grimes and Jack Johncey (Butt of Bourton).

MORETON HORSE SHOW in 1933 with Mr A. Bluck's successful team of shire horses, headed by 'Weston Avon Mischieful', winner of the Colt Foal class. Still an important event in the local calendar (and one of the biggest one-day shows in England), the modern Moreton Show began in 1949 although its origins go back through the three societies incorporated at that time: the Moreton Horse Show, Moreton Agricultural Society and the Cotswold Agricultural Society.

JUDGES AND OFFICIALS at Moreton Show in 1938, themselves a group of well-known local farmers: Harold Shepard of Barton-on-the-Heath (see page 36), -?-, William Timms of Old Farm, Dorn, (?) Thomas Merrill of Blenheim Farm, Moreton, Charles Dee of Park Farm, Blockley, Thomas Slatter of Broadwell and -?-.

OPENING OF THE NEW BRITISH LEGION CLUB for Moreton on 30 September 1933 in Station Approach by General Sir Francis Davies of Elmley Castle near Pershore (third from left). The old club, a wooden hut in Station Road, was used by Moreton Scouts until replaced by a stone building.

ANOTHER OPENING, this time of the new WI Hall in March 1954, 33 years after an institute was started in the town. From the left : Mrs Beardsmore, Mrs Goode, Mrs Curtis, Miss Sollis, Mrs Grimwood, Mrs Barkes, Mrs Currill, Mrs Gray, Mrs Horne, Mrs Drury, Mrs Rolph, Mrs Tarplett, Mrs Norledge, Mrs Bunt, Miss Gray and Miss Clements (*Evesham News & Journal*).

# Villages around Moreton:
# Todenham
# Adlestrop
# Broadwell
# Donnington
# Longborough
# Condicote
# Sezincote
# Bourton-on-the-Hill
# Batsford

TODENHAM CLUB on parade in 1914, the first of several photographs in this album recording Cotswold village feast days. Whitsun was the traditional time for Club Day, a celebration within living memory in many villages where a particular day was always associated with each place. A church parade, feast and fair were the main highlights. Clubs were village friendly and dividend societies, providing basic insurance against loss of income during illness in the days before national schemes.

THE HOME GUARD at Todenham in 1940. Back row: Mr Walters, Clem Skilton, Jim Meadows, John Meadows and Eric Forge. Middle row: Alf Randall, Jack Slatter, Eric Bishop, Albert White, Harry Stanley and Harold Gilson. Front row: air raid wardens Hubert Mann, Ernest Webb, Stephen Randall and Frank Reeves with Womens Land Army member Dorothy Savage.

Lower End, Adlestrop.

LOWER END at Adlestrop, typically Cotswold and here with a strong estate influence. The pair of cottages in the centre of the picture carry the Leigh family crest and the date 1868 (Clift & Ryland of Stow).

ADLESTROP PARK, owned by the Leigh family from 1553. The major feature of this Victorian photograph is the Sanderson Miller-designed Gothic style dating from the rebuilding of 1759–62 – a fine façade.

LOYAL SUPPORTERS OF VILLAGE CRICKET at Adlestrop in 1925 (Frank Packer of Chipping Norton).

A COTTAGE AT ADLESTROP on the line of the old road via Adlestrop Bridge across the river Evenlode. This was altered in 1803 as part of the laying out of Adlestrop Park. Adlestrop railway station was later built across the old line of the road (Frank Packer of Chipping Norton).

SISTERS ALICE AND AGNES PHILLIPS aged 8 and 11 at their home in Adlestrop around 1908. The photograph was taken in a strawberry patch!

ADLESTROP STATION in two views taken on the same day in the early 1930s by Chipping Norton photographer Frank Packer. Together they form a fine record of this rural station on the London–Worcester line a few miles from Moreton (page 20). This particular station is of course best known for the lines in Edward Thomas' poem and indeed three staff seems an over supply for such a rural place. Opened in 1853, Adlestrop survived until January 1966, but its heyday as part of the Great Western Railway was already at its height when these photographs were taken. The station house survives and one of the station nameboards is preserved on display in the village.

BROADWELL VILLAGE seen in a set of four photographs from the Packer studios at Chipping Norton. The village lies half a mile from the Fosse Way and part of its charm is a village green, seen above and below on the right and the left respectively. Below and across to the left is Pimlico Row which was built (?rebuilt) in 1858 and partially demolished in 1959.

THE FOX INN on the left is the survivor of Broadwell's two pubs; its rival the Wheatsheaf closed over 70 years ago. On the right is Griffin Hill.

ANOTHER VIEW OF BROADWELL VILLAGE which derives its name from the largest of the several springs in the vicinity. Broadwell Farm is on the left.

BUILDING DUNCOMBE HOUSE in Donnington parish in 1919; the wooden and rope-lashed scaffolding seems alien to the modern eye.

GARDEN FÊTE at Donnington Manor on 29 June 1921, one of a set taken on the occasion by the Butt Studio of Bourton (and Stow).

LONGBOROUGH VILLAGE is set on rising ground and its centre is dominated by the church of St James which has fine details from the fourteenth and fifteenth centuries. The tower is thirteenth century. The lower view shows Church Street (upper picture J.W. Farrell, Stow-on-the-Wold, and lower F. Norman, printer, Cheltenham).

A SPLENDID VIEW, postmarked 1915, with a group of village children. A few years later this was to be the site of the Longborough war memorial (page 55). The building on the left is the Coach & Horses pub.

IN THE LANE OFF BANKS FEE LANE. Alf Green, the village lamplighter, lived in one of these cottages (postmarked 1910).

AT THE ASHWELL SPRING in Longborough, sometime after the rebuilding and raising of the wall in 1914/5. Ashwell is thought to commemorate a thirteenth-century place name, although its other name was the Laurels, an obvious link with the walnut, chestnut, yews and laurels in the area behind. At one time the spring fed the whole village and farmers could fill up their water carts here. In this view are village children Harold Clarke and Olive Webb with either Sidney Eastbury or Williams on the wall (J.W. Farrell, Stow-on-the-Wold).

THE READING ROOM, now village hall, in Longborough High Street, was built in 1904 in memory of Frederick Brooke Dugdale VC, a survivor of the Boer War but the victim of a hunting accident in 1902. The elaborate door and surround is modelled upon Upper Swell Manor. The original trust deed allowed only for men to use the facilities of the room to read newspapers and play billiards (J.W. Farrell of Stow-on-the-Wold).

A VIEW OF THE VILLAGE from the Ganborough road (Frank Packer of Chipping Norton).

CUTTING A WAY THROUGH on 3 April 1916 after a deep snowfall on 28 March which was the heaviest recorded fall since 1881 (J.W. Farrell of Stow-on-the-Wold).

BANKS FEE, the core of one of the two Longborough estates which have existed since the thirteenth century. The name is an extraordinary survival of a personal name over seven centuries, for the manor was in the hands of the Lebanc family by 1220. Fee may relate to a reward for service to the king. The house is of 1753, replacing an earlier building (Frank Packer of Chipping Norton).

UNVEILING LONGBOROUGH'S WAR MEMORIAL on 30 April 1921. Compare the scene with Moreton a month earlier (page 25) and Campden in January (page 145), (Butt of Bourton).

A LONGBOROUGH FÊTE on 8 July 1929, another village show recorded by the Butt studio of Bourton.

PEAPICKERS in Mr Stokes' field at Lower Sand Furlong in 1936. From the left: Millicent Honour, Cissie Newman, Mrs Newman, Alice Joynes and Mrs Gardner, with Dolly Gardner in the foreground. The Newmans kept the Coach & Horses pub in Longborough and later the Golden Ball at Lower Swell before returning to live in Longborough.

CHARLIE YOUNG and his wife Mary in retirement at Hope Cottage, Longborough. Charlie was a horsebreaker and died in 1952 at the age of 91. Mary died in 1961 aged 93 (*Evesham Journal*).

FÊTE AT BANKS FEE around 1960. From the left Leon Brookes, Miss Foster, Miss Glady Burford, Ron Brookes, May Brookes and Beattie Brookes.

TWO VIEWS OF THE CENTRE OF CONDICOTE VILLAGE around the wall-enclosed village green. The wayside cross is fourteenth century and beyond is the small church of St Nicholas, of the twelfth century but badly 'scraped' when it was restored a century ago. The postcard with the upper view carried a brief message when it was posted on Saturday 28 August 1915 : 'Making a round of Winchcombe and back' (James Alden, Stow-on-the-Wold).

TWO VIEWS showing both the laying of the foundation stone for the new chapel at Condicote and the party assembling for the opening ceremony of the completed building. The dates are 19 April and 28 June 1911 respectively. The chapel had a short life, closing in 1921, although the Home Guard used it during the Second World War ('R.A.').

SEZINCOTE is one of the Cotswolds' most individualistic houses, built in the Indian style of the early nineteenth century for Sir Charles Cockerell whose family had made its fortune in the service of the East India Company. The entrance front is surmounted by a central onion-shaped dome whilst the greenhouse wing frames the garden layout. Skilful detailing owed much to the Indian topographical artist Thomas Daniell who advised during construction. Much of Sezincote can be claimed to have inspired the Brighton Pavilion of the Prince Regent following his visit in 1807 (Butt of Bourton).

IN THE GROUNDS OF THE HOUSE an open-air performance of a Shakespearian play on 22 June 1926, when Sezincote was the home of Col. and Mrs Arthur Dugdale (pages 27 & 37). In the audience is the Revd W.L. Warne, whose brief history of nearby Moreton-in-Marsh remains a valuable local record.

PICNIC at Sezincote Warren in June 1911.

SEZINCOTE FÊTE organising committee on 31 August 1921 (Butt of Bourton and Stow).

BEEHIVE LODGE – suitably named – at Sezincote or Bourton Hill Stud on the main road from Stow to Broadway. The building survives but sadly minus its splendid thatch and with a new chimney. The gates have also disappeared (Chapman & Co. Blockley).

Bourton-on-the-Hill (looking down).

A PAIR OF VIEWS of the main street of Bourton-on-the-Hill astride the main road west from Moreton (the modern A44). These are charming studies and carefuly posed for Clift & Ryland of Stow-on-the-Wold. The church of St Laurence stands very close to the road in the centre of the village (upper view postmarked August 1911).

Bourton-on-the-Hill (looking up).

STONE QUARRY at Bourton-on-the-Hill, one of a large number of Cotswold quarries being worked for building stone as well as for roof slates, dry-stone walling and road-making. Quality varied from quarry to quarry with building stone being extracted in blocks and then sawn by hand into shape. Few now survive, although evidence of this important Cotswold industry is not difficult to find (Percy Simms of Chipping Norton, Four Shire Series).

FLOWER SHOW at Bourton-on-the-Hill, undated (Frank Packer of Chipping Norton).

ALGERNON BERTRAM FREEMAN MITFORD, born 1837 and created Baron Redesdale in 1902. He had succeeded to Batsford Park in 1886 (page 12) and undertook the major rebuilding work. He died in 1916 and was succeeded by his son the Hon. David Mitford as the second baron.

BATSFORD PARK, almost entirely rebuilt between 1888 and 1892 by the first Baron Redesdale. This aspect overlooks the gardens (J.W. Farrell, Stow-on-the-Wold).

LORD REDESDALE with his stallion 'Chance', London Champion in 1882 and sold in 1885 for 520 guineas.

BATSFORD PARK was a hive of activity during the 1880s and subsequent years. Following his inheritance in May 1886, Algernon Bertram Freeman Mitford set about the major rebuilding of Batsford Park on a grand scale. The style is Cotswold Elizabethan on an E-shaped plan and built in a golden ashlar. The entrance front presents an impressive aspect and commands a fine view of the landscape. Apart from the house, the gardens are also notable and include an arboretum designed and planted by the owner, fired with inspiration from his posting to the British Embassy in Tokyo. He created a Japanese element within an English setting.

Mitford's career had been as a diplomat in Russia and China as well as Japan. At home he had been Secretary to the Board of Works, with responsibility for periods of restoration at Windsor Castle, Hampton Court and the Tower of London. He resigned these duties to take up his inheritance at Batsford.

The stable block also dates from this period (1878). It provided a base for the development of the Batsford Shire Stud, set up with John Timms one of the estate tenants, whose son William became a most successful stud manager. Although the stud was sold in 1897, one legacy of this period was the Moreton Shire Horse Society started in 1889, and one of the precursors of the present-day Moreton Show (page 39).

Some of this activity is recorded by the camera of the Hon. David Mitford, son and heir who succeeded as the second baron on his father's death in 1916. He was a keen photographer who developed and printed his own work in a darkroom at Batsford Park (page 14). The photograph above is probably one of his, taken at the gates to the big house and showing the attractive lodge. The scene is obviously posed, but nevertheless has a distinct appeal with an excellent example of a local farm wagon and its horse team acting as focal point. The lady in the doorway wears a traditional bonnet.

ANOTHER VIEW OF THE SAME PLACE with the estate's Kerry cattle on view. The lady in the bonnet still lurks in the lodge doorway.

A MAJOR EVENT in this period was the visit of the king in July 1905 (page 21). The bunting is out in Batsford village as the royal party is awaited. Righton's delivery van is pulled up at the roadside (postmarked 1907).

ANOTHER FAMILY PHOTOGRAPH on the estate, possibly at Downs Farm, and showing a horse team harrowing.

A TROLLEY made in the estate workshops by Philip Pulley (on left) for Sir Gilbert A.H. Willis Bart., who had bought Batsford Park from the second Baron Redesdale in 1919 (page 25). He was created Baron Dulverton of Batsford on 8 July 1929, which dates this photograph between 1919 and 1929. The carter is Harry Savin (Butt of Bourton).

HAYMAKING on the Batsford estate about 1895. On the right is Algernon Freeman Mitford and the photograph is almost certainly another taken by his son. At this time, the horses would have formed part of the Batsford Shire Horse Stud. The small tree in the bottom left is now over 180ft. high!

# SECTION THREE

# Blockley

BLOCKLEY CHURCH, seen here in an undated photograph recovered from the cellars at the Devizes office of the *Wiltshire Gazette & Herald* and identified following an appeal in that newspaper. The unknown photographer seems to have visited Blockley on a Cotswold tour. He would have found a pleasant village – large by village standards but too small to be classed as a town – and one which, until 1931, was in Worcestershire.

It owes much of its distinctive modern appearance to its period of prosperity as a centre for silk mills. In the eighteenth and early nineteenth centuries there were no less than 11 mills on the Blockley Brook and its tributary the Cole Brook, an area particularly suited to the process of silk 'throwing' with an ample and never-failing supply of pure water containing just enough lime to give a sheen to the washed silk. The process consisted of washing and preparing the raw silk for the ribbon weavers of Coventry. In 1824 eight mills were at work employing about 300 women and children with up to 3000 working at home within a ten-mile radius of Blockley. But the business fluctuated and then collapsed after the ending of restrictions upon the rival French market in 1860. By 1885 this collapse was complete.

The subsequent history of the mill buildings is varied and many survive. On the left in this photograph is Mill Close, an eighteenth-century building (?1714) which made a later claim to fame as the Astral Works, where a water turbine produced sufficient electrical power to light the church, the vicarage, the school and the street – and thus allow Blockley to become of the first villages in the country to have electric light. As the Village Institute, it suffered a fire in 1931 and was rebuilt (page 88).

THE SQUARE, BLOCKLEY, C. 1887, with George Herbert's ironmonger's and general house furnisher's shop on the right (now Church Gates). This picture is the work of George Evans, portrait and landscape photographer of Tallow Hill, Worcester.

THE SQUARE looking towards the church of St Peter & St Paul in August 1901.

FANCY DRESS PARADE along St Georges Terrace.

BLOCKLEY'S IMPRESSIVE ELM TREE at the top of the village, felled in January 1952 (Chapman of Blockley).

HIGH STREET C. 1912, from a greetings card. This street retains a fine group of eighteenth-
and nineteenth-century houses, and has an additional attraction in the number of raised
footpaths. Richard Belcher (front cover) had six of these in Blockley fenced 'with substantial
iron posts and rails' in the middle of last century as work for the unemployed in the winter
months. On the left is the Crown Hotel.

HIGH STREET AGAIN, this time looking in the opposite direction (J. Lucking, late Chapman & Co. Blockley).

BLOCKLEY BUTCHER MR BALHATCHET with his Christmas display c. 1930, a remarkable exhibition and something of a Blockley tradition. It is said that a night watchman was employed to guard the display overnight.

HIGH STREET, bedecked for the Jubilee of Queen Victoria in 1887 and waiting for the procession. One of Blockley's early electric street lights can be seen on the post to the left (Chapman & Co. Blockley).

JOYNER'S 'wholesale and retail family grocery, wine and spirit and provision establishment' on the right c. 1890, which produced an advertisement extolling the benefits of electric lighting for its customers. On the left the Bell Inn coach house was the original Blockley school and at this time also housed the fire engine.

CHAPEL GATES C. 1905 and the entrance to the chapel on the front cover of this album. On the left is Sirett's photographic shop, undoubtedly the source of many of Blockley's fine collection of historical views. The gentleman on the left with boater and bicycle was Mr Sirett sen., Baptist minister at Cutsdean.

THE MAN HIMSELF, CALEB SIRETT in c. 1910 on a postcard labelled 'C. Sirett, Photographer & Stationer, Blockley, Worcs'.

A WEDDING CELEBRATION at the Ebenezer Baptist Chapel with carriages awaiting the happy couple. In the picture are Dennis and George Rouse, Mr Webb and Mr Payne.

A GENERAL VIEW OF BLOCKLEY with the school of 1867 (now Admiral Collier Centre) in the foreground. High Street is conspicuous and so too the Baptist Meeting House of 1794 on Bell Bank. It has been the village hall since 1925 (Butt of Bourton).

GOOD FRIDAY MEETING of representatives of chapels in the district, outside the Ebenezer Chapel in the High Street in 1932. On display is the Shield of Honour of the Cotswold Sunday School Union for Scholars in Scripture by Examination. Sporting a buttonhole on the right of the front row is Cecil Wilkins, a well-known Baptist from Bourton-on-the-Water. At bottom left is Mr Joyner and behind the man with the shield is Miss Warner (?Butt of Bourton).

FARM WORKER CHARLES WILCOX of Rose Row, Blockley, using an aero or seed fiddle. Time consuming and laborious, this method often supplemented mechanical drilling.

UPPER HIGH STREET C. 1922 with Mr Bennett's horse and cart prominent. On the bank behind the cottages stands a house used at times for refuge by Joanna Southcott, the Blockley prophetess, during the period 1804–14.

GLEANING or 'leasing' from the fields supplemented the income of country people, with the bundles of corn sold to the miller for modest sums. The old lady in this group is Mrs 'Trotty' Eastbury.

FISH COTTAGE at the Dovedale end of High Street and home of a local legend, a long-lived pet trout for whom a memorial reads :

'In memory of the old fish
Under the soil
The old fish do lie
20 years he lived
And then did die
He was so tame
You understand
He would come and
Eat out of your hand
Died April the 20th 1855
Aged 20 years.'

GREAT FIRE in Blockley High Street on 2 March 1926, one of several large fires in the village over the years. The pump is the horse-drawn hand-pump later replaced by the engine on page 31.

CLEARING UP after an earlier fire at the post office next to chapel gates in the High Street, 1907 (Chapman & Co. Blockley).

DEVASTATION AT DOVEDALE HOUSE on 31 August 1925, with fire hoses still running across the garden and smoke rising from the end section of the house which was not rebuilt (Frank Packer of Chipping Norton).

IN DOVEDALE WOODS. High Street leads into Dovedale, offering an enchanting walk close to the centre of Blockley. Its landscaping – from Blockley Wood – formed part of the second Lord Northwick's improvements to his estate in the nineteenth century (C. Sirett, Blockley Photographic Series).

HENRY SALE, for many years parish verger, who died at the age of 86 in December 1950. The standard history of Blockley speaks of him as 'born, bred and honoured in Blockley'. His wife died on the day of his funeral.

WILLIAM HOWELL and his family ran a specialised business manufacturing heavy-duty cask hoops made from the butts of ash poles, which were used in the Black Country chain industry for the transport of chains and other heavy goods in manageable loads. They also made hurdles (stacked up in the lower picture), ladders and gates. The family moved to Moreton in 1918 and carried on the business until 1963. William Howell was also something of a local poet. These views date from 1910 and show (above) the recently widowed Howell with his children, Charles, Ernest, Annie, Alice and Harry. Below, J. Webb, general haulier of Blockley, is collecting a load for the station.

THE GROUND FLOOR AND BASEMENT of Edwin Smith's mill of c. 1714 was used by the Blockley Electric Lighting Co. from 1887 until 1931. It was from here – as the Astral Works – that the village enjoyed early electric light. In this photograph c. 1898 workmen are converting the first floor into the Village Institute which also survived until 1931 when the building was severely damaged by fire. It was rebuilt and is now Mill Close (lower photo: 'R.A.P. Co. Ltd').

Church and Institute, Blockley.

88

LOOKING TOWARDS LOWER STREET with the fine stand of trees forming the 'twelve apostles' on the right.

LOWER STREET AGAIN, c. 1900, with Colebrook mill and mill house on the left (Chapman & Co. Blockley).

PARADE, outside the Great Western Arms Inn in Station Road, of the Great Western Sick & Dividend Club, the banner of which records its establishment in 1897. Club day here was the Wednesday of Whit week and Blockley brass band is in attendance. Earlier friendly societies had included the Blockley Benefit Society – the 'Old Club' – and the Victoria Friendly Society (Chapman, Sirett & Co. Photo Artists, Blockley, Worcs).

THE BRASS BAND is here too at an unidentified and undated gathering which might be another Club day, with the ladies and children lined up for the photographer (C. Sirett, High Street, Blockley).

VIEWS OF TWO MORE BLOCKLEY PARADES of the GWA Sick & Dividend Society, the lower picture outside Joyner's shop. This is a different (? and later) banner, although still recording the establishment of the society in 1897. The lower view is believed to date after 1912 and before 1928 when fire damaged the house in Bell Lane just to the right of the banner.

LADY EDWARD SPENCER-CHURCHILL opening the fête at Blockley Court, formerly Westmacott's or Marlborough mill, which was converted into flats in 1925 (Frank Packer, Chipping Norton). The lower view is believed to be the same occasion.

MOTHERS' MEETING on 14 July 1909 from a postcard sent a few days later : 'Dear Mother, Should be glad to have Hetty's little cream dress for Sunday if possible. This is the Mothers Meeting tea taken at Higgins. You will recognise some. Much love, Kitty' (Chapman, Artist, Blockley).

WOMENS INSTITUTE at a gathering a few years later. Note the misspelling on the caption.

ANOTHER BLOCKLEY WOMEN'S MEETING, on 26 May 1936 (Butt of Bourton). Compare the fashions with the previous two photographs.

BLOCKLEY OVER 60S CLUB at its (?formation) meeting in 1955, lined up for the photographer outside Cromwell Terrace.

WI ANNUAL SUPPER held on 25 October 1957.

CAPTAIN EDWARD GEORGE SPENCER-CHURCHILL was 'squire' of Blockley for half a century from 1912 and endowed the community in a number of ways. The Bowling club was presented with a new green alongside the church c. 1914 (Chapman & Co., Blockley).

STALWARTS OF THE BOWLING CLUB in a group photograph probably taken some years before the presentation of the new green. Perhaps about 1903?

Years later Capt. Spencer-Churchill – as club president – again performs the honours at the opening of the Northwick Club bowling green in September 1960 (*Evesham Journal*).

NORTHWICK PARK, one of the major houses of the North Cotswolds which, in its Victorian heyday, enjoyed all the style of country house life. Several building periods can be seen in the façades of the house. This view, a century or so ago, shows the south front of 1828; to the left is the early eighteenth-century orangery, and on the right the picture gallery extension which was added in 1832. The Northwick family were squires of Blockley and surrounding villages for over 200 years (Hartwell, High Street Broadway).

THIS LATER VIEW shows the main (east) entrance to the house on the occasion of a meet of the North Cotswold hounds. The house was famous for its picture collection which was housed in the extension (J. Jacques, jun., Broadway).

UPPER SERVANTS of Northwick Park, including, seated on the left, Miss Pugh the housekeeper.

A CHILDREN'S PARTY AT NORTHWICK PARK watched over by Lady Northwick from her invalid carriage. The donkey is 'Cleopatra'. Widow of the third Lord Northwick who died in 1887, Augusta Lady Northwick was head of the family estate until her own death in 1912 (Chapman & Co., Series, Blockley).

FUNERAL PROCESSION for Lady Northwick (aged 80) on 1 June 1912, a memorable day in the history of Blockley. Mr George Tustin is driving the first carriage (J. Lucking (late Chapman & Co.) Blockley).

THE SPLENDOUR OF THE PICTURE GALLERY in 1954 with Capt. Spencer-Churchill posing with his family collection. Following his death a decade later, the collection was dispersed at auction, arousing widespread interest in the break-up of the estate and the ending of a family link with Northwick dating back to the late seventeenth century.

ONE OF CAPT. SPENCER-CHURCHILL'S ESTABLISHMENTS was the Northwick Brick & Tile Works near the railway station, set up as an employment measure after the First World War. Skeletons of Saxon date were discovered by workmen in 1925 which inspired a poem by the local 'Draycott poetess' Lily Webb. From the left, Morris Eastbury, Fred Fairbrother (from Todenham) and Fred Hale.

BLOCKLEY STATION opened on the Oxford–Worcester line in 1853 with a ceremony where 'about 2000 people were hospitably entertained'. This view shows the original wooden OW & W station buildings (Chapman, Artist, Blockley, Worcs).

HAYMAKING AND RICK-BUILDING at Park Farm, Blockley, in July 1906; a fine scene of agricultural activity. The wagon is a local 'box' type.

# North Cotswold Villages:
# Aston Magna & Draycott
# Paxford
# Ebrington
# Hidcote & Mickleton
# Weston-sub-Edge
# Aston-sub-Edge & Saintbury
# Willersey

ASTON MAGNA BRICK & TILE WORKS alongside the railway line near Moreton-in-Marsh, taken from a promotional postcard used by sales representatives. Just as the nearby Northwick works had been set up to create employment (page 101), so Lord Redesdale established the Gloucestershire Brick Co. in 1901.

DRAYCOTT MISSION HALL, an undated study of a simple building by Moreton-in-Marsh photographer S.A. Freeman.

OX-ROAST at Draycott as part of the 1953 Coronation festivities on 2 June. The beast was dressed and prepared by the staff of Drury's butchers of Moreton-in-Marsh, whose men here are Archie Grieve and William Dyer, the latter a direct link with the pre-war ox-roast scenes from Moreton on page 38. Sporting rosettes are Arthur Gladwin and Walter Hodkins (Butt of Bourton).

PAXFORD CHAPEL: another, albeit modest, reminder of the Baptist persuasion in the area. It opened in 1836 (Chapman & Co. Series).

OPENING OF PAXFORD WORKMEN'S INSTITUTE – or club room – on 25 February 1910. It served village needs for a number of years and after a period of disuse was restored in 1979 by local volunteers (Chapman, Sirett & Co., photo artists, Blockley, Worcs).

OLD MANOR HOUSE, divided into farm labourers' cottages.

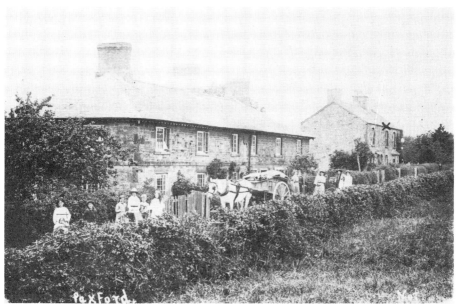

THE OPPORTUNITY TO BE PHOTOGRAPHED is not missed by this group of Paxford women and children.

MOTHER AND (?)DAUGHTER outside a Paxford cottage. Can they be identified?

PAXFORD FC. winners of the Bourton Hospital Cup in 1928–29. Compare this with Moreton FC on page 35, winners of the same cup two seasons later (Butt of Bourton).

MAYTIME CELEBRATIONS in Paxford in 1929: a revival from an earlier tradition and held on the Saturday nearest to 12 May. In the centre is Sam Bennett, the well-known fiddler from Ilmington and on the right the schoolteacher Mrs Bennett (Butt of Bourton).

MAY DAY COMMITTEE for the Paxford celebrations of 12 May 1931. From the left in the back row: Algy Bagnall, Jim Beazley, Lewis George Heath (the local county councillor), Harry Fisher, George Cother, Bill Plummer and Fred Bagnall. In the front: Bert Taplin, Harry Newman, Frank Kyte, Joe Stinton and Ernie Stinton – for these last two see page 33 (Butt of Bourton).

CELEBRATING MAYTIME AGAIN, on this occasion during the early 1950s. Children perform a maypole dance (*Evesham Journal*).

PAXFORD'S OLDEST VILLAGER MRS COX — in her late eighties — hands out 1953 Coronation mugs to village children from her cottage doorway. From the left: George Boulter, Muriel Harris and her brother Colin, Rita Harris, Fred Bagnall and Mrs C. Smith (Mrs Cox's daughter) and on the right Mildred Griffin, great-grandaughter of Mrs Cox. Continuity indeed!

WORKSHOP of the long established Paxford family business of Keytes, wheelwrights and carpenters. The last Cotswold wagon made in these workshops a century ago was celebrated in Edith Brill's *Life & Tradition on the Cotswolds* (new edition 1987). Village wheelwrights frequently doubled as general carpenters and undertakers, and many surviving rural undertakers businesses can trace their origins back to the building of farm wagons and carts last century. Traditional methods often survived undisturbed in this environment; Keytes continued to cut timber by hand in their saw-pit until 1926 (photo courtesy of Peter Turner).

PLENTY OF THATCH IN EVIDENCE in these views of Ebrington's main street c. 1900. Note the ricks between the cottages and the pump alongside the lane. The cottages below right were demolished to make way for the Church Close housing development. Town Farm is bottom left.

ALONG THE VILLAGE STREET with Home Farm to the right (Percy Simms Four Shire Series).

EBRINGTON CLUB forming up for its Whit Thursday procession. Here there are three banners, the main one plus one each with the arms of the Lords Harrowby and Fortescue, the two major landowners of the village. At Ebrington the holiday extended to three days.

CLUB BANNER of the Ebrington Friendly Society, formed on 29 September 1856, adorned with the legends 'Let Brotherly Love Continue' and 'Unity is Strength'. There is a strong similarity with trade union banners in both design and slogan (*Evesham Journal*).

VILLAGE BAND in 1903, atop one of the village farm wagons.

PLOUGHING MATCH around the turn of the century at Ebrington; an opportunity not only for companionship and entertainment for the farming community but also for assessment of the latest ploughing equipment. Such matches also offered publicity for manufacturers and suppliers.

TWO GATHERINGS C. 1900 of Ebrington villagers. Above is a club day gathering in the yard of the Ebrington Arms. The gentleman on the left bears a striking resemblance to one in the previous picture. Below is the Mothers Union meeting at the vicarage. Second and fourth from right respectively are Mrs Mary Lloyd and Mrs Drinkwater.

BY THE FIRESIDE of the Ebrington Arms, which was originally a seventeenth-century farmhouse. Note the drinking mugs and the furniture.

ALFRED RASTALL, retired carter from Ebrington, at the age of 84. He lived to be 96 years of age.

HIDCOTE BARTRIM MANOR, a seventeenth- and eighteenth-century house, seen here from the courtyard. On the left is a barn converted into a chapel earlier this century with traceried windows from elsewhere. Now a property of the National Trust, Hidcote is best known for its gardens laid out by Laurence Johnston.

THE ENTRANCE TO CAMPDEN OR MICKLETON TUNNEL and the only one on the railway line between Paddington and Worcester. Half a mile long, it is part of Campden Bank, a long descent for trains running off the Cotswolds towards Worcester and a spectacular spot in the days of steam. Here a maintenance gang have possession of the line.

MICKLETON VILLAGE SCENES, with the stone construction of the Cotswolds mixed with brick and thatch as building material. Indeed Mickleton is at the very edge of Gloucestershire and usually regarded as the northernmost Cotswold village. Below, the smithy buildings survive as a shop; the house behind is Holly Mount (upper photo F.C. Rickett, Stratford-upon-Avon, and Claverdon 'The Mercia Series').

WESTON-SUB-EDGE as its name suggests is also at the Cotswold edge with the vale of Evesham, the village straggling down the hill to meet the main road from Cheltenham to Stratford. Quieter days are recorded outside the village pub at the junction above, whilst the influence of the growing tourist market can be detected in the captioning of the scene below as 'picturesque cottages'. Interestingly, both postcards are produced by Stratford-upon-Avon publishers, F.C. Rickett and 'Antona' respectively.

ASTON-SUB-EDGE village hall and war memorial.

SAINTBURY CROSS, probably fourteenth century in date, stands 11ft. high. The sundial head and cross were added in 1850. Amongst medieval preaching crosses, Saintbury is unusual in standing so far from the church which is higher up the hillside ('Antona' series).

WILLERSEY market gardener Charles Andrews and his wife c. 1900 outside the Church Street cottage where they lived for 30 years. His produce in the baskets included asparagus whilst the rush basket or frail contained his provisions for the day. Photographed by the rector Revd C.O. Bartlett.

# SECTION FIVE

# Chipping Campden

*Market Cross. Chipping Campden*

CHIPPING CAMPDEN HIGH STREET and its buildings must be one of the archetypal English street scenes, regularly used for souvenir calendars and publications. In fact, the preservation of Campden is tightly protected and controlled, owing not a little to the discerning influence of incoming residents as much as local people over the years. Before the development of mass tourism with its consequent 'prettification', Campden's main streets resembled any other small English market town with a variety of activities caught within this series of photographs.

Turn of the century Cotswold towns often looked much less well preserved, polished and presentable than today's versions and Campden was no exception. However good the quality of the surviving buildings, only constant care can preserve them and investment in this asset has not always had the priority now demanded by present-day society.

Campden had such a particular influence exerted upon it with the arrival of the Guild of Handicrafts from London in 1902; some 50 members had a considerable effect, not least in the restoration of a number of Campden buildings. This tradition was continued with the foundation of the Campden Trust in 1929 by F.L. Griggs and others, and still leaves its mark.

Pride of place in the Campden street scene must go to the Market Hall in the centre of the High Street. It was built by Sir Baptist Hicks in 1627 for the sale of cheese, butter and poultry, and the Hicks family coat of arms can be seen in the small central gable. Preserved in its original state, the hall has been owned by the National Trust since 1944.

This view also shows the Town Hall beyond, originally fourteenth-century, but largely rebuilt in the nineteenth-century. The porch was added in the year of the 1897 Jubilee celebrations of Queen Victoria (Walker of Stratford-upon-Avon).

LOOKING IN THE OPPOSITE DIRECTION along the southern side of High Street and at an earlier date. On the immediate right is Percy Prout's drapers and outfitters shop, later Elsley's ironmongers. Beyond, the hanging sign of the Live & Let Live Inn.

INSIDE THE MARKET HALL with the cobbled paving clearly in evidence.

OLD GRAMMAR SCHOOL on the south side of High Street. A foundation of the fifteenth century, the school has a long and distinguished history as one of the oldest schools in the country. This façade dates to the rebuilding of 1865, and the school moved out to new buildings at the north end of the town in 1927. On the right is part of Elsley's shop (page 129).

CAMPDEN GRAMMAR SCHOOL PUPILS in an undated photograph.

CAMPDEN SCHOOLCHILDREN in form IV at Easter 1910. Can any be identified ?

THE BAND OF CAMPDEN GRAMMAR SCHOOL CADET FORCE in 1919. The buglers are L. Horne, C. Mace, H. Purser, C. Clemmett, E. Organ & G. Cole, the kettle drummers A. Leech, A. Cooper and S. Picton, and the big drummer E. Williams.

THE STORES OF T.W. COLEMAN, which was a 'family grocers, tea dealer, Italian warehousemen and provision merchants' with advertising to match. It seems appropriate that this site later became a supermarket. The building is Badger's Hall of seventeenth-century date.

HARRY PITCHER, Campden postman and parish councillor.

'ELSLEY, LATE HORNE, IRONMONGER & SEEDSMAN' in the High Street, taken in 1909.

EXTERIOR OF THE LYGON ARMS HOTEL, catering for both a family and commercial clientele. The good quality signwriting is unusually large on the stone façade of a Cotswold building. The word 'Garage' has replaced 'Good Stabling' over the arch.

AN OVERSIZE LOAD OF STRAW makes an unusual picture of the Bedford Pick-up of Ebrington haulier S. Drinkwater in Campden High Street.

MRS DICKENSON, whose husband Bob achieved local fame for stopping King Edward VII's car in Broad Campden in 1908 to sell him a newspaper. Thereafter he carried a version of the royal crest on his sack. The enamel sign outside his house advertises his business.

GREVEL'S HOUSE is another of Campden's significant buildings, dating from c. 1380. Its owner, William Grevel, was one of England's most influential woolmen and a financier for King Richard II. He died in 1401. Originally set around a courtyard, the open hall rose to the full height of the house.

LOOKING INTO LEYSBOURNE from High Street with a good mix of building styles.

THIS VIEW OF THE ALMSHOUSES AND CHURCH in Church Street is another favourite Campden scene. It owes much to the town's major benefactor, the first Viscount Campden, Sir Baptist Hicks, who built the almshouses in 1612. A London merchant who accumulated a large fortune under King James I, Hicks settled in Campden and built himself a mansion, also completed about the same time. Its entrance gateway can be seen in the distance.

THE ALMSHOUSES ARE STILL OCCUPIED, and have been regarded by one authority as 'the crowning achievement of the domestic Cotswold style and mason-craft of the early seventeenth century'. They were restored in 1953. In the foreground is the town's old cart wash, itself now a period piece.

ALMSHOUSE RESIDENTS in the late 1920s or early '30s: -?-, -?-, Mrs Cheory, Bill Cheory, Long Tommy Bennett, -?-, Mrs Keen, John Keen (formerly a shoemaker), -?-, Harry Weaver, -?-, Mrs Weaver and Joe Baker.

MRS POLLY WAIN, a well-known Campden lady, outside her almshouse. She died in 1934.

AT WORK IN CHURCH STREET is this ten-ton steam roller made by Bomford & Evershed of Salford Priors, Evesham. Is it engaged on road work for the county council?

CHURCH GATES, CAMPDEN.

WELL WORTH A SECOND LOOK, this view of Church Street allows the setting of the parish church of St James to be appreciated. The fine perpendicular detailing of the tower indicates its status as one of the classic 'wool' churches of the Cotswolds, exhibiting both internally and externally a unity of fifteenth-century design.

It is offset nicely by the lodges and gateway of the Campden mansion which stood in its own grounds behind the wall to the right. This house was short-lived; it was destroyed during the Civil War in 1645 and only a short section of the frontage survives, together with two pavilions and the entrance gateway above.

Also of interest is the thatched cottage, seen at its gable-end in this photograph. Whilst so much around it has been preserved, this cottage was demolished between 1951–56.

NORTH AND SOUTH LODGES at the entrance to the mansion, providing a fine study of Jacobean style, and suitably restored with the advice of F.L. Griggs of the Campden Trust c. 1930. The church steps are on the left.

WEST BANQUETING HALL, one of the two pavilions which completed the design of Hick's mansion. Probably built as summer houses, they have principal rooms on the level of the terrace. The twisted chimney stacks are an interesting detail.

EAST BANQUETING HALL. Compare the detailing with the previous photographs.

CHURCH COTTAGES, one of which was a black-smith's workshop. The inevitable fire risk has taken its toll on this group too (R.A. Postcards Ltd).

THE VICARAGE just west of the church. One of the two Victorian extensions to this eighteenth-century house has since been demolished and the stone used to build nearby Little Glebe (Taunt & Co., No. 1575, postmarked 30 March 1907).

CAMPDEN CHURCH INTERIOR, showing the fine symmetry of this great 'wool' church (Chamberlain, Campden).

COURT FARM, with its barns and shelter sheds tucked into the remaining buildings of the old Campden house. To the right can be seen one of the lodges from page 136 and, in front of the church tower, the rear of the thatched cottage in Church Street (page 135). Otherwise this is a very typical farmyard scene of the 1920s, a mixture of tile and thatch with an excellent example of a Cotswold harvest wagon in the yard. The dove or pigeon loft adds a further point of interest (courtesy John Topham Picture Library).

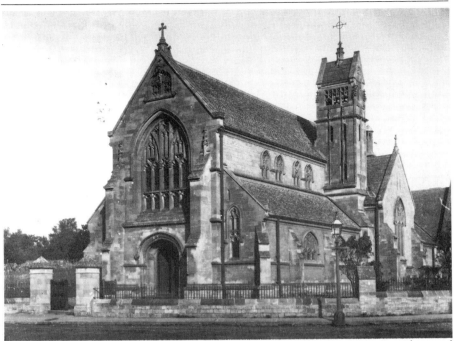

CHURCH OF ST CATHERINE built in 1891 for the Roman Catholic community in and around Campden. It stands in Lower High Street and was largely paid for by the third Lord Gainsborough.

FATHER BILLSBOROUGH, priest to the Catholic community and a great cricketer.

POST OFFICE STAFF for Campden, photographed about the turn of the century. Was this taken in the garden of the post office at London House in the High Street and is the central figure at the rear a younger version of the Harry Pitcher on page 128?

BASKETMAKING in Harry Ellis' workshop in 1911, on a site now occupied by Campden Vintners.

COL. LYNCH-STANTON photographed outside his home at The Court House, another surviving part of the old Campden house and possibly originally its stable block.

FLORAL FESTIVAL PARADE through the High Street, a big event in the town's calendar and part of the Whitsuntide Wakes celebrations up until the First World War (Chapman & Co., Blockley).

CAMPDEN MORRIS MEN remain one of the few sides to preserve a 'traditional' dancing style within the Cotswold variations of dance. Here a newly-revived side contribute to the Floral Festival on 25 May 1896 – six dancers, a fiddler and a fool (H.W. Taunt of Oxford).

'THE BIDFORD SHAKESPEARIAN MORRIS DANCERS' as promoted on the posters for the 1896 Festival. Taken on the same day, this side parades amongst the ruins in the grounds of old Campden house (H.W. Taunt of Oxford).

PIG ROAST in 1918 in front of Smith's butcher's shop with Charlie Ladbrook in the white smock. From the right : Arthur Bradley, Arthur Brotheridge, Alfred Blakeman, Jack Aspin, Horace Buckland, 'Old Bright', Jim Payne, Bob Dickenson (page 130), Mrs Bob Newman, Lewis Smith and Tom Hopkins.

WAR MEMORIAL unveiling on 9 January 1921 on a site between the Town Hall and the Market Hall. The memorial was designed by F.L. Griggs (T. Elsley, Campden).

SCUTTLEBROOK WAKE in Leysbourne, seen here between the wars. In effect the town's carnival, the Wake consists of a procession and fair, morris dancing and the crowning of the Scuttlebrook Queen. The name derives from an open stream which ran down the middle of Leysbourne until culverted in 1831.

JUBILEE PROCESSION 1935 passing the Town Hall led by George Ebborn, chairman of the parish council, and Harry Pitcher, clerk. Harry Ellis carries the 'Volunteers' flag and the riders are Sylvia Gabb and Stella Warden.

ANOTHER OX-ROAST, this time on 12 May 1937 (Butt of Bourton).

CAMPDEN JUNIORS contributing to the Tewkesbury Music Festival on 16 March 1937.

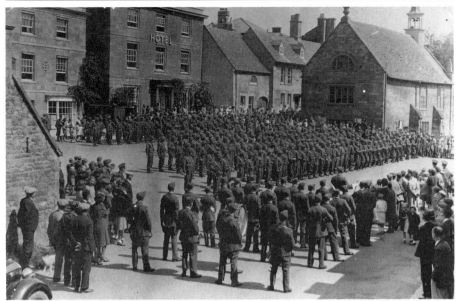

MILITARY PARADE, probably the departure of the Green Howards who had been billeted in the town from December 1939. The kilted figure on the left below suggests the incoming Gordon Highlanders who also enjoyed Campden hospitality for a period. The RAF detachment is from Moreton or Honeybourne (W. Dennis Moss of Cirencester).

WILLIAM HEDGES, a shepherd from Campden who was born c. 1834 at Hannington, Wiltshire. In the 1881 census he was living at Westington and had six sons. In 1909 Cecil Sharp collected a dozen folk songs from him when he was aged 76 (Museum of English Rural Life).

FAIR DAY in the Market Square: a suitable point to note the derivation of the word Chipping in the town's name as *ceping*, a market or market-place. Campden was an important centre for sheep sales, which enjoyed pride of place in the town centre whilst at this time cattle and pigs were sold in a paddock at the rear of one of the main hotels. The fair was held on the last Wednesday of each month (Frank Packer of Chipping Norton).

PRISONERS OF WAR at work on the land near Chipping Campden during the First World War. Are any other details available?

ROSE COTTAGES at Westington.

THE HAYDEN FAMILY outside the smithy at Forge Cottages, Westington, in 1903.

CYCLING PARTY at the corner of Leysbourne with Cider Mill Lane. The sign advertises Parsons & Son (later Wilmot's) plumbing business. The building has a date stone of 1847.

BUILDING DOVER'S COURT in the late 1920s for F.L. Griggs, artist and designer, who had moved to Campden in 1904 and was a leading advocate for the preservation of the town's buildings and its character. He was much involved in the formation of the Campden Society in 1924 and the Campden Trust in 1929. In Dover's Court he achieved his ambition of building a traditional Cotswold house in correct local materials and with the best craftsman from local builders Pyments.

THE OWNER OF THIS MATCHLESS MOTOR BIKE poses to good effect against the backdrop of the Market Hall.

JACK HORNE with his local bus taking up a very similar pose. Horne is one of the longest established Campden family names.

CAMPDEN STATION, an early twentieth-century view which compares with nearby Blockley, the next station on the line (page 101). Both were opened in 1853 and closed in 1966, Campden retaining most of its original buildings and layout until the end.

Campden House.

CAMPDEN HOUSE, or New Campden House to distinguish it from Hicks' mansion in the town. In fact Hicks did own the original Jacobean house standing on its own in the valley at Combe in 1628. However, for much of its history it is associated with the long-standing Campden family of Noel, created Earls of Gainsborough in the early Victorian period. The first earl rebuilt on a large scale in 1846 and this is the house seen above on a Chapman of Blockley postcard. When the estate was broken up in the face of death duties in the late 1920s, the new owner engaged architect Norman Jewson to reshape the house as the more recent view shows.

WESTINGTON QUARRIES above Campden were the source of much of the stone from which the town was built (and rebuilt). In fact stone was mined as well as quarried as the above photograph by Henry Taunt of Oxford shows, c. 1895. The mine entrance is on the left. In this century J.W. Strange & Sons ran the quarry for a number of years and below, in the 1950s, father James Strange unloads a new block whilst son John (front left) moves a dressed slab. At the rear is Dick James, a quarryman. The range of buildings is typical of a quarry of the time (courtesy *Sunday Mercury*).

CHARLES BLAKEMAN, alias 'Slap', one of Campden's characters, seen here in typical pose. He sold walking sticks and attended local events such as Ebrington Club.

STEAM THRESHING on a winter's day by the Badger family at Lapstone Farm.

It seems suitable to conclude with another example of a Cotswold village custom already seen elsewhere in these pages ... the village club parade and feast. Here Chipping Campden Band are ready to lead off the parade of Mickleton Club, behind a large and very fine banner. Just visible are the brass stave-heads of the Club, carried on poles in the procession and a symbol of the traditions of village clubs. The policeman in attendance seems to be sharing a joke with the bandsmen. Although the crowd may have been small, this scene typifies much of the tradition of Cotswold village life in the years before the First World War.

# ACKNOWLEDGEMENTS

This volume was planned as a companion (and to some extent a sequel) to my *Northleach to Stow-on-the-Wold In Old Photographs* (1987) in the same series, and the material selected here complements the photographs in that volume. In each case, the chosen area is within both Gloucestershire and indeed the local government boundaries of Cotswold District Council. This allows for compactness and also leaves open the opportunity for future volumes on those parts of the Cotswolds stretching into the surrounding counties of Oxfordshire, Warwickshire and Worcestershire.

The compilation of such a volume required the support and guidance of a great many people, acting both individually or on behalf of local history groups and societies. I have been welcomed without hesitation wherever my temerity has led me, for which I express my sincere thanks. It has been no easy task to build captions around such a wealth of photographic material without in some degree risking errors in my knowledge of the detail of local history. Such errors will surely exist for which I both apologize and appeal to be corrected. A reference copy together with a full list of the sources of photographs used in this volume will be maintained at the Cotswold Countryside Collection museum of rural life at Northleach as part of that institution's archive of Cotswold history.

Most of the Moreton-in-Marsh and Batsford pictures have been drawn from the collections of the Moreton-in-Marsh & District Local History Society, with the generous assistance of Mrs Catherine Meadows of Lower Lemington. The debt owed to the late Reg Drury has already been acknowledged on page 6. The local Moreton knowledge and postcards of Guy Stapleton and Lionel Jones (now of Cheltenham) proved invaluable, as did once again the advice and sound guidance of David Day, whose contacts in the north Cotswolds proved to be many and helpful. As before, he has generously contributed the Introduction to this album, thus setting its course from the outset. Margaret Shepard made available both Longborough photographs and local knowledge, allowing that village to have a 'good innings' in these pages, for which thanks are also due to Miss Gladys Burford and Mr Aubrey Honour. For Blockley, Dr Arthur Exell gave both hospitality and wisdom in my search through the fine collections of the Blockley Antiquarian Society, the source of most of Section Three.

I approached Section V for Chipping Campden with some trepidation, concerned to do justice to that delightful place. I need not have worried as both Horace Haines and family at Westington and Pat Thomson in Back Ends gave generously of both time and information. Access to the Don Ellis collection of Campden photographs proved invaluable. My quest through Adlestrop and Broadwell was guided by Janet Walker of Adlestrop and through Paxford by Joy Grove, now of Cheltenham. Other pictures came from Phil Griffiths of Cirencester and the collections of the Museum of English Rural Life at the University of Reading and the Oxford City Library. The *Wiltshire Gazette & Herald* kindly rehabilitated a group of Cotswold subjects following the identification on page 72.

Lastly, and by no means least, many of these photographs have been taken from the collections of the Cotswold Museums Service at Cirencester and Northleach and thanks are due to Cotswold District Council for this opportunity and to the many donors of material. In particular I would like to thank all the staff of the Corinium Museum at Cirencester and the Cotswold Countryside Collection at Northleach for their support during the preparation of this (and earlier) volumes, and for their enthusiasm for the preservation of this aspect of Cotswold history. Both to them and those mentioned above, I hope that this album is a small token of endeavour.

David Viner
Cotswold Countryside Collection
Northleach
1 September 1988.